On the Front Line

IN THE TRENCHES IN WORLD WAR I

Adam Hibbert

Raintree

Chicago, Illinois

First published in Great Britain by Raintree, © Copyright 2006 Raintree
Published by Raintree,
a division of Reed Elsevier Inc.
Chicago, IL 60602

Customer Service 888-363-4266
Visit our website at www.heinemannraintree.com

For more information address the publisher:
Raintree, 100 N. LaSalle, Suite 1200, Chicago, IL 60602

Produced for Raintree Publishers by Discovery Books Ltd
Editorial: Kathryn Walker, Juliet Smith, and Daniel Nunn
Expert reader: David Downing
Design: Rob Norridge, Michelle Lisseter, and Clare Nicholas
Picture research: Amy Sparks
Project manager: Juliet Smith
Production: Duncan Gilbert
Printed and bound in China by South China Printing Company Ltd
Originated by Dot Gradations Ltd

10
10 9 8 7 6 5 4 3 2

Library of Congress Cataloging-in-Publication Data
Hibbert, Adam, 1968-
    In the trenches in World War I / Adam Hibbert.
       p. cm. -- (Freestyle express) (On the front line)
    Includes bibliographical references and index.
    ISBN 978-1-4109-2194-9 (lib. bdg., hard. : alk. paper) --
    ISBN 1-4109-2194-8 (lib. bdg., hard. : alk. paper) --
    ISBN 978-1-4109-2201-4 (pbk. : alk. paper)
    ISBN 1-4109-2201-4 (pbk. : alk. paper) 1. World War,
    1914-1918--Juvenile literature. I. Title. II. Series. III. Series:
    On the front line
D522.7.H53 2006b
940.4--dc22
                                    2005029245

This leveled text is a version of *Freestyle: On the Front Line: In the Trenches in World War I*

Original edition produced by White-Thomson Publishing Ltd, Bridgewater Business Centre, 210 High Street, Lewes BN7 2NH, United Kingdom.

Acknowledgments
The publishers would like to thank the following for permission to reproduce photographs:
AKG pp. **14–15, 16,** 17(r), 24(r), **32, 36,** 38(b); Corbis pp. **13,** 14(l), 15(r), **21, 26, 27, 31, 33, 40;** Harcourt pp. **title page,** 4–5, **7, 8,** 12(l), **20,** 23(r), 34–35, 37(t), 37(b), 38(t); Popperfoto p. **18;** Topfoto pp. **9, 11,** 12(r), 17(l), 19(l), 19(r), 24(l), 25, 28(l), 28–29, 30, 35, 39, 41.

Cover photograph of soldiers of the Royal Irish Rifles in the trenches during the Battle of the Somme in 1916 reproduced with permission of AKG.

Maps on pp. 6, 10 by Peter Bull.

Every effort has been made to contact copyright holders of any material reproduced in this book. Any omissions will be rectified in subsequent printings if notice is given to the publishers.

The paper used to print this book comes from sustainable resources.

CONTENTS

Any words appearing in the text in bold, **like this,** are explained in the glossary. You can also look out for them in the Word Bank box at the bottom of each page.

OVER THE TOP

The Great War

World War I began in 1914 and ended in 1918. It was the first war to involve many countries around the world. Because of this, it became known as the "Great War." More than eight million soldiers died in the war.

It was September 1915. World War I had been going on for thirteen months. Patrick MacGill was a British soldier. He was fighting at Loos in northern France.

At Loos the British and German armies had dug long, narrow holes in the ground. These were called **trenches**. Trenches gave soldiers shelter from enemy bullets.

The British attack

The British were preparing for a major attack on the enemy **lines**. MacGill's job was to help wounded soldiers.

These British troops are leaving the safety of their trenches to go "over the top." This meant facing enemy gunfire. A **shell** has just exploded to their right. ➡

Word Bank   trench long, narrow hole in the ground

British guns fired at the Germans for four days. On September 25, the British soldiers climbed out of their trenches. They moved toward the German soldiers. This was called going "**over the top.**"

A horrible sight

MacGill was horrified by the scene outside his trench. Men were walking through gunfire, smoke, and poison gas. Wounded men were crawling on the ground. Parts of bodies lay everywhere. MacGill lost count of the number of dying men he cared for that day.

Find out later

Why were trenches built in a zigzag pattern?

Do you recognize the German soldier with the moustache?

How did the Germans use dogs like this one in the trenches?

line lines of trenches and other defenses

HEADING FOR WAR

Battleships

Britain controlled the seas with its **fleet** of warships. But in the early 1900s, Germany began building a fleet to compete with Britain's. This made many British people think that Germany was looking for a fight.

At the start of the 20th century, there were five powerful nations in Europe. These were Britain, France, Germany, **Austria-Hungary**, and Russia.

These five powers competed with each other. They competed both in Europe and around the world. They competed for the right to sell their goods in foreign markets. They competed for raw materials (such as oil or metals). They competed for power in Africa and Asia.

All this competition created more and more bad feeling. There was a growing fear of war.

This map shows the countries of Europe during World War I. It also shows which side each country was on in 1915. →

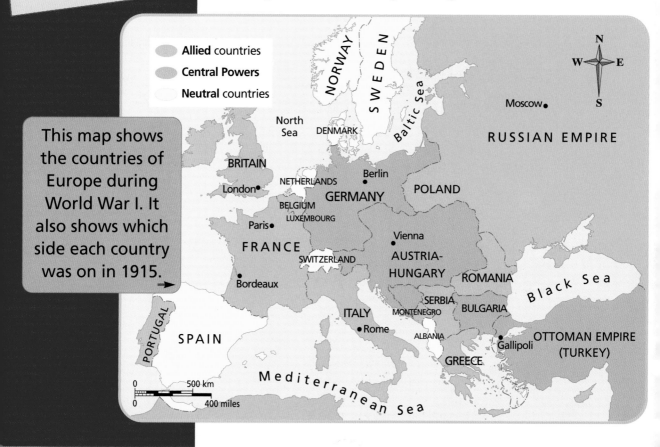

- **Allied** countries
- **Central Powers**
- **Neutral** countries

NORWAY · SWEDEN · Baltic Sea · Moscow · RUSSIAN EMPIRE · North Sea · DENMARK · BRITAIN · Berlin · POLAND · London · NETHERLANDS · GERMANY · BELGIUM · LUXEMBOURG · Paris · Vienna · FRANCE · AUSTRIA-HUNGARY · SWITZERLAND · ROMANIA · Black Sea · Bordeaux · SERBIA · MONTENEGRO · BULGARIA · ITALY · Rome · ALBANIA · OTTOMAN EMPIRE (TURKEY) · Gallipoli · PORTUGAL · SPAIN · GREECE · Mediterranean Sea

0 500 km
0 400 miles

Word Bank   fleet group of warships, or an entire navy

A web of promises

Four of the five powers formed **alliances**. France and Russia promised to help each other if either was attacked. Germany and its neighbor, Austria-Hungary, did the same.

Britain had promised to defend Belgium if it was **invaded**. Belgium is a small country between Germany and France. If either France or Germany attacked the other through Belgium, Britain would become their enemy.

War fever

People had been expecting war for many years. In 1914 Britain, Russia, and France went to war against the **Central Powers**. The Central Powers at this time were Germany, Turkey, and Austria-Hungary. Thousands of young men rushed to join their country's army.

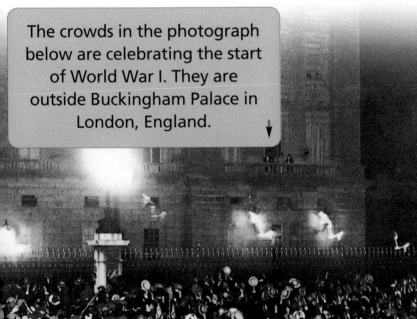

The crowds in the photograph below are celebrating the start of World War I. They are outside Buckingham Palace in London, England.

alliance   two or more countries that have agreed to help each other in wartime

Reasons for war

There were many reasons why World War I began. They included:

• countries competing for rich **resources**

• national pride

• lots of different countries agreeing to help each other

• the murder of Archduke Franz Ferdinand

• many mistakes made by leaders

The shot that sparked a war

On June 28, 1914, a man named Archduke Franz Ferdinand was shot and killed. The archduke had been chosen to be the next ruler of **Austria-Hungary**.

Europe moves toward war

The archduke was shot by a Serb named Gavrilo Princip. The country of Serbia lay on the southeastern border of Austria-Hungary (see the map on page 6). Austria-Hungary blamed Serbia for the killing. It threatened to **invade** Serbia.

Archduke Franz Ferdinand and his wife Sophie sit in the back of their car. Minutes later, they were both shot. →

Word Bank   invade enter a territory with armed forces, often to conquer that territory

Serbia was a friend of Russia, so Russia prepared for war. Russia's action forced Germany and France to prepare for war. This was because of the promises the powers had made to help each other (see page 7).

Germany's plan

If war broke out, Germany would have to fight France in the west and Russia in the east. Germany had a plan for defeating France quickly, before Russia was ready for war. This plan involved going through Belgium.

On August 3, 1914, German troops crossed the Belgian border. The following day, Britain declared war on Germany.

Armed strength

By 1914, countries all over the world had thousands of soldiers ready to fight.

Germany	850,000
Austria-Hungary	430,000
France	750,000
Russia	1,500,000
Britain	120,000
Britain's Empire	170,000
Belgium	43,000
Japan	75,000
United States	25,000

The German ruler, **Kaiser** Wilhelm I (standing in front of the flag) receives news about his troops before the outbreak of the war in 1914.

resource useful material, such as oil or metals

THE BATTLE RAGES

The battle areas of France and Belgium became known as the **Western Front.** British troops joined the French to fight the Germans. France, Britain, and Belgium together were called the "**Allies**" (see the map on page 6).

Rapid advance

The Germans forced the Allies back. German troops quickly moved through Belgium. They then moved into northern France. The German army was soon close to Paris, the French capital.

Battle of the Marne

On September 6, 1914, **Allied** troops fought the Germans near the Marne River in France.

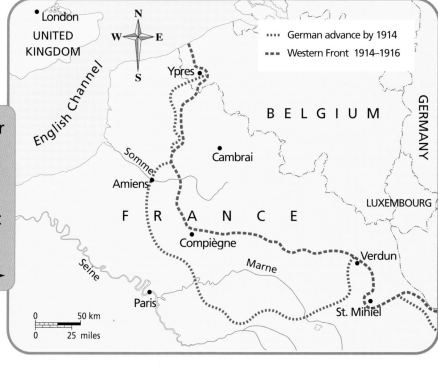

This map shows how far the Germans **advanced** in 1914. It also shows the location of the Western Front for most of the war between 1914 and 1916. ➡

Word Bank   advance move forward

At the Battle of the Marne, the Allies forced the German army to **retreat**.

A line of trenches

The Germans and the Allies began to dig long **trenches**. They fought each other from these trenches. By late December 1914 the line of trenches was 500 miles (800 kilometers) long. The line ran from the sea in the north to the Swiss border in the south (see the map on page 10).

No-man's-land

When two enemy armies dug trenches, there was a space between them. Neither side controlled this space. It was called **no-man's-land**. Anyone in no-man's-land was an easy target. No-man's-land was full of big holes made by explosions.

These Allied troops have dug into a trench in northern France. ➡

retreat move back

The world sends troops

Nelson and Frederic Scrivener lived in Queensland, Australia. Australia was part of the **British Empire**. The brothers wanted to help Britain in the war. They joined the Australian army.

In 1915 the brothers were sent to the Greek island of Lemnos. At Lemnos, they prepared to fight the **Ottoman Empire**. The Ottoman Empire was Germany's ally. Its center was modern-day Turkey (see page 6).

Going to the trenches

Many countries sent troops to fight alongside the **Allies**. These included:

Countries	Soldiers
Australia	322,000
Canada	418,000
India	70,000
New Zealand	100,000
South Africa	33,000

The poster on the near right encourages young British men to join the army. The poster on the far right appealed to men throughout the British Empire to join the war. ➡

BRITONS
"WANTS"
YOU
JOIN YOUR COUNTRY'S ARMY!
GOD SAVE THE KING

THE EMPIRE NEEDS MEN
THE OVERSEAS STATES
All answer the call.
Helped by the YOUNG LIONS
The OLD LION defies his Foes
ENLIST NOW.

Word Bank   British Empire group of countries once controlled by Britain. In 1914, it included 25 percent of the world's land area.

Brothers into battle

The attack on the Ottoman Empire began in April 1915. **Allied** troops landed at Gallipoli in northwestern Turkey. A bullet hit Nelson in the leg as he landed on the beach.

Nelson was sent to a hospital. Fred stayed on. His job was carrying stretchers and helping the wounded. Both brothers were lucky. They survived the war.

A huge crowd of people gather in Melbourne, Australia. They are saying good-bye to Australian troops leaving for the war in Europe.

Ottoman Empire large area of southwestern Asia, northeastern Africa, and southeastern Europe. Modern-day Turkey was at its center.

Trench design

On the **Western Front,** both sides dug complicated networks of **trenches**. These trenches could shelter an entire army.

The trenches were usually deeper than a tall man. There was a ledge on the front wall called a "fire step." Soldiers would step onto it to fire rifles over the edge of the trench.

The front trench was built in a zigzag line. This was so that an enemy entering the trench could not shoot along it.

This German trench near Verdun in France (see the map on page 10) can still be visited today. You can see how the trench zigzags.

These British soldiers are resting in a trench on the Western Front. British trenches were muddy, cold, and wet. They often collapsed and buried the soldiers inside.

Word Bank   Western Front battlefront between Germany and France

Communications trenches

Communications trenches ran between safe areas and the front-line trench. They allowed troops to move safely to and from the front line.

Dugouts

Soldiers could rest in rooms cut into the walls of the trenches. These rooms were called **dugouts**. The **Allies** built rough dugouts because they expected the battle **lines** to move. The Germans built comfortable dugouts, designed for longer use.

Sandbags

Sandbags are cloth bags filled with sand or earth. A wall of sandbags could stop bullets. But explosions easily knocked over the sandbags. They always needed repairing. Sandbags were mostly used where it was too difficult to dig the ground.

This German trench on the Western Front was more comfortable than the British trenches. It had rooms to sleep in and wooden floors.

Allies countries, such as Britain, France, the United States, and Russia, that fought together against Germany in World War I

Trench repairs

Pierre Jacard was an **engineer** in the French army. In 1915 Jacard lived close to the Verdun **trenches** (see map on page 10). Every night, Jacard and his team went into the front-line trench.

Jacard's team carried wooden beams and planks for trench repairs. These were also used for propping up the roof inside **dugouts**.

French soldiers take a short rest. They are repairing their defenses at Verdun, France. The year is 1916.

Word Bank   engineer   person trained to build and repair things

Different jobs

Whenever Germans attacked the front line, Jacard's team had lots of work to do. Jacard had to repair the trenches. At night, he and his team had to put up barbed-wire fences in **no-man's-land**. Barbed wire prevented the enemy from entering the trenches.

Telegraph wires ran between the trenches and the headquarters. These wires were often broken by exploding bombs. Jacard's team had to work hard to keep the lines working.

Bird's-eye view
Both sides sent people up in balloons or aircraft to spy on the enemy. The German balloon below was used to spy on the British **lines**.

Telegraph wires were not the only way of communicating between trenches and headquarters. German troops used dogs to carry food and messages.

telegraph   simple telephone that uses beeps for signals rather than voices

LIFE IN THE TRENCHES

Bill Turner was a British soldier. On Christmas Day 1914, he was in a **trench** near Ypres in Belgium (see the map on page 10). The day before, there had been fierce fighting between the British and German soldiers.

But on Christmas morning, Turner heard German troops singing. The Germans showed their heads above their trenches. Then a German soldier walked toward Turner's trench. Turner did not shoot him because the German had no gun.

These British soldiers are celebrating Christmas Day in a **shell** hole. There is a soldier's grave nearby.

Word Bank   no-man's-land   unclaimed area of land separating enemies

Brief truce

The brave German talked with the British soldiers. They agreed to stop fighting until 4 P.M. Both sides would go into **no-man's-land** and bury their dead.

When they were in no-man's-land, the enemies sang together. They even played soccer together. At 4 P.M. they went back to their trenches. This friendliness never happened again.

German soldiers take a break from the bitter fighting to play a game of soccer.

Adolf Hitler

North of Ypres, one young man was angry about the Christmas **truce**. His name was Adolf Hitler (below right). He was a corporal in the German army. Within twenty years, Hitler would be leader of Germany.

truce temporary agreement to stop fighting

Basic survival

William Peden was a Canadian soldier. He arrived in France early in 1915. Then he moved on to Ypres in Belgium.

Terrible conditions

Digging **trenches** at Ypres was hard. The ground in Peden's part of the **line** was very muddy. The soldiers' feet were always wet. This caused a condition known as "**trench foot.**" A bad case of trench foot could cause the skin of the foot to rot. This could even kill a soldier.

A British soldier in a water-filled trench.

Word Bank   trench long, narrow hole in the ground

Thousands of dead soldiers were buried in the wet ground. Sometimes digging new trenches uncovered the bodies.

A lucky wound

Peden was "lucky." He was shot in the hand at Ypres in 1915 and needed hospital treatment. He went to Britain to recover. Many soldiers wished they would get a wound like this. Peden survived the war.

A way to escape

"Lucky" wounds like Peden's allowed a soldier to spend a long time away from the horror of the trenches. Sometimes soldiers injured themselves on purpose so they could leave the trenches. But if they were caught, they could be put in prison for two years with **hard labor**.

Food and other supplies were carried through the trenches. Feeding thousands of troops in awful conditions was very difficult.

hard labor   punishment that involves hard, physical work

Digging for survival

Otto von Borries was a German soldier. In June 1916 he was near Serre in northern France. His commander wanted shelters cut into the hillside. Von Borries helped dig these shelters.

The Battle of the Somme

At the end of June, British **artillery** began pounding the German **trenches**. Von Borries and his friends hid in a shelter for six days. Then the gunfire stopped. A guard yelled: "Get out! They're coming!" Von Borries scrambled out and set up his machine gun.

Thousands of soldiers were wounded in battle. Here, Canadian troops take care of captured German soldiers who are wounded. The picture was taken in September 1916. ➡

Word Bank   artillery large guns that fire shells or missiles

Deadly surprise

The British thought their heavy fire had killed all the German soldiers. British soldiers were walking toward the German trenches. But von Borries and his friends were alive and ready to fight. Their shelters had saved their lives.

The attack was a disaster for the British. About 60,000 British soldiers were killed or wounded on the first day of the Battle of the Somme.

War in the air

In World War I, aircraft fought for control of the skies above the battlefields. But the aircraft were not as good as modern-day planes. These planes could not change the outcome of the war.

The photo below shows mechanics of the British Women's Royal Air Force (WRAF) working on a World War I plane.

WAR ACROSS THE WORLD

In August 1914 Germany failed to defeat France quickly on the **Western Front**. It now had to fight the Russians in the east as well. This battlefront was called the **Eastern Front**. Germany had to divide its forces between the two fronts.

At war with Russia

In mid-August Russian armies **invaded** the northeastern corner of Germany. This area was called East Prussia. At the end of August, the Russians were defeated in a battle at Tannenberg. German troops destroyed part of the Russian army.

Women and the home front

Many men left their jobs in factories to fight in the war. All through Europe and America, women had to do the men's jobs. The women in the photo below are making **ammunition** for the war.

German soldiers **advance** on the Eastern Front in 1915.

Word Bank   Eastern Front   battlefront between Germany and Russia

Farther south, Russia and **Austria-Hungary** were fighting each other. They were fighting for control of the Carpathian Mountains. These mountains lay on the border between the two countries.

Russians driven out!

The Russian army was huge. But Germany and Austria-Hungary had better supplies of guns and **shells**. In the summer of 1915, Germany forced the Russians to **retreat** hundreds of miles (kilometers).

The Russian army sent millions of soldiers to the Eastern Front to hold back the German army.

ammunition   bullets, shells, mines, and bombs

The Gallipoli campaign

In November 1914 the **Ottoman Empire** (see map on page 6) entered the war on Germany's side. At that time, Russia was fighting both Germany and **Austria-Hungary**. The **Allies** decided to attack the Ottoman Empire. They hoped this would take pressure off Russia.

The Allies decided to **invade** Turkey, the center of the Ottoman Empire. They aimed to capture the channel of sea called the Dardanelles. The Dardanelles is the entrance to the Black Sea.

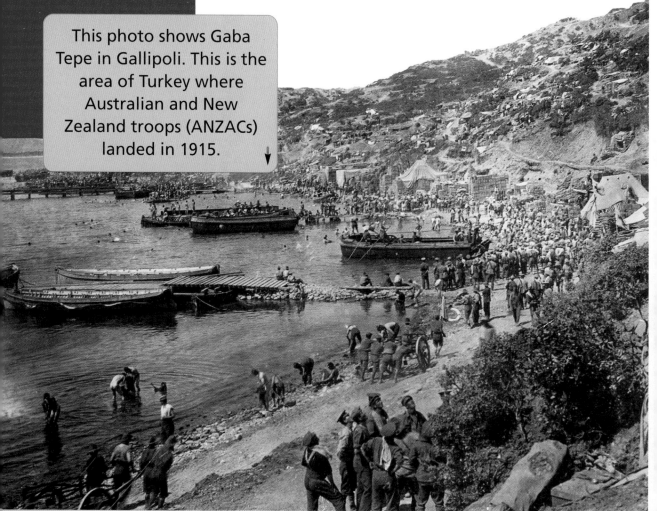

This photo shows Gaba Tepe in Gallipoli. This is the area of Turkey where Australian and New Zealand troops (ANZACs) landed in 1915.

Word Bank   Allies countries, such as Britain, France, the United States, and Russia, that fought together against Germany in World War I

On April 25, 1915, **Allied** troops landed on the beaches of the Gallipoli **peninsula** in Turkey. The Australian and New Zealand Army Corps (**ANZACs**) joined the British and French troops.

The battle is lost

But the Allies could not push back the Turkish forces. The invasion soon came to a stop, and soldiers dug **trenches**. By November the Allies realized they were losing. In December 1915 the Allies left the area. Many lives had been lost on both sides.

ANZAC troops charge uphill during the Gallipoli campaign in 1915. They are fighting Turkish forces for control of the high ground.

Gallipoli time line

February 19, 1915 – The Allies bombard the coast of Turkey.

March 18 – Allied battleships attack the Turkish coast.

April 25 – ANZACs and others storm the beaches at Gallipoli.

May 19 – Turkish troops attack the Allies.

June 28 – The Allies begin to make a small **advance** against the Turkish troops.

November 15 – The Allies realize they are losing and decide to leave.

December 20 – The last ANZACs leave in boats.

January 9, 1916 – The last **Allied** troops leave Gallipoli. The **campaign** is over.

campaign series of military operations during a war, all with the same purpose

INDUSTRIAL WAR

Mahomet Fidale was a soldier in the French army. On April 22, 1915, Mahomet was at Ypres in Belgium. At about 5 P.M. a cloud of smoke rose from the German **trenches**. The French thought an attack had started. Fidale began shooting.

Poison clouds

But this smoke was unusual. The cloud was green. It drifted across **no-man's-land** toward Fidale. Suddenly, there was panic. It was not smoke. The Germans had released **chlorine** gas.

These French soldiers are wearing **gas masks**. They are waiting for a gas attack.

This famous painting by John Singer Sargent shows soldiers blinded by mustard gas.

Word Bank chlorine greenish yellow gas that can kill people

Panic!

Fidale's lungs began to burn. His eyes streamed with tears. Some soldiers ran away. But Fidale stayed in his trench until the gas cloud blew past him. Fidale survived. But many breathed in too much gas and died.

Canada saves the day

In the panic that followed the gas attack, the Germans attacked. But Canadian troops rushed to hold the **line**. They drove the Germans back.

Types of poison gas

There are many types of poison gas. They include:

- Tear gas – This gas feels like pepper in the eyes and throat. It has no lasting effects.
- Mustard gas – This gas causes burns, severe pain, and blindness.
- Chlorine and **phosgene** – These gases make the lungs fill up with fluids. Victims "drown" to death.

gas mask face mask with filters to remove poison gas

An attack on Verdun

Ernst Krieg and his brother Erich were German soldiers. In 1916 they were near Verdun in France (see map on page 10).

Verdun was famous for its **fortresses**. These strong buildings had been designed to defend the area against attack. The Germans guessed that France would use all its soldiers to defend Verdun. If the Germans kept attacking Verdun, France could lose huge numbers of soldiers.

German guns hammered the French army for days. On February 21 the guns stopped.

(see map on page 10)

Army police

After a charge began, army police searched their own trenches. They looked for soldiers who had failed to attack. On the **Western Front**, about 1,000 British and French soldiers were executed for refusing to fight.

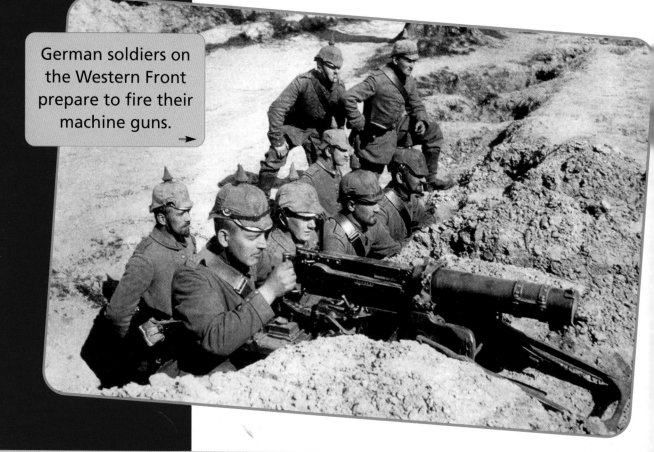

German soldiers on the Western Front prepare to fire their machine guns.

Word Bank   fortress specially strengthened building designed to defend an area in wartime

Thousands of Germans pushed forward. Ernst and Erich lost each other.

Surviving to fight another day

Ernst made it to the first French **trench**. Then he and his friends moved forward through machine-gun fire and **shells**. That evening, the Germans dug in. Ernst and Erich found each other safe.

The battle lasted until December 1916. The French took back almost all the ground that Erich and the others had fought for.

This photo shows the conditions that French troops lived in during the Battle of Verdun in 1916.

The Battle of Verdun

The Battle of Verdun lasted from February to December 1916. Almost one million people were killed or wounded.

February 22, 1916 – The Germans take the first French trenches.

March 6 – The French hold back a German **advance** at Mort Homme hill.

June 7 – The Germans take Fort Vaux.

July – The Germans shell Fort Souville with **phosgene** gas.

October 24 – The French regain positions.

November 2 – Fort Vaux is retaken by France.

phosgene   colorless poison gas that can kill people

War underground

Joseph Henry Hollow was a bit too old to be a fighting soldier. But he was fit, strong, and brave enough to tunnel. He was a tunneler with the Australian army.

In September 1916 Hollow was working near Messines in France. He and twelve others were digging through soggy **clay** with shovels. They were slowly digging toward the German **lines**.

Dangerous work

Tunnelers made noise as they scraped through the dirt. If they were heard, they were in danger. Enemy soldiers could drill holes above them. They could drop explosives to blow up the tunnelers.

A French tunneler tests a switch. This switch will set off explosives at the end of the tunnel. The explosives are under the enemy.

Destroying the Messines Ridge

Hollow's tunnel took over a year to finish. It ran under the Messines **Ridge**. The German army on the ridge was heavily defended. Also, this was a difficult position to attack. Hollow and his team placed **mines** under the ridge.

Success!

Just after 3 A.M. on June 7, 1917, the explosives went off. The blast woke people hundreds of miles (kilometers) away in London. The German lines were destroyed. Nearly 10,000 Germans soldiers died.

French **trench** diggers come out from a tunnel. They had been digging under German lines in July 1916.

The Cambrai Offensive

On November 20, 1917, German troops in Cambrai got a nasty shock. Cambrai is in France (see the map on page 10). At 6:20 A.M. the **Allies** launched an attack with their new tanks. Hundreds of tanks drove over German **trenches**.

The attack forced the Germans to move back many miles (kilometers). At first it looked as if the Allies had beaten Germany back. The attack was called the Cambrai Offensive.

(see the map on page 10)

Cambrai time line

November 20, 1917 – The Allies attack. They break the German **line**.

November 23–28, 1917 – The Allies take Bourlon Wood. This is the most important high ground in the area.

November 30, 1917 – Germany fights back.

December 4, 1917 – The Allies lose all the ground gained and more.

Tanks at Cambrai advance slowly toward the battlefield. On their roofs they carry bridging bundles to help the tanks cross trenches.

Word Bank   advance move forward

Germany fights back

The Germans began to fight back on November 30. The Germans **advanced** in small teams. Each team fought alone. But other teams following behind stopped them from being surrounded by the enemy.

Many British soldiers were almost cut off. Some generals had to scramble to escape. The Germans captured over 200 **Allied** tanks. By December the Allies had lost all the ground they had gained.

War at sea
Neither side won the battle at sea. But the British navy trapped the German navy inside the North Sea. The main sea battle was the Battle of Jutland. It took place in the North Sea (see map on page 6). Neither side won. Britain lost more ships, but the German **fleet** was still trapped.

Bridging bundle

A British battleship fires its guns during the Battle of Jutland in 1916.

Allied belonging to the group of countries that fought together against Germany in World War I

Zimmerman telegram

In January 1917 the Germans sent a telegram to Mexico. British spies got hold of it. The telegram said that Germany would support Mexico if it invaded the United States. This became known as the Zimmerman telegram, named after the German minister who sent it. The telegram convinced many Americans that Germany was their enemy.

In February 1917 Germany decided its submarines would sink any ship bringing supplies to Britain and France. This meant that German submarines would sink U.S. ships delivering goods to Britain.

Enter the United States; exit Russia

Germany's attacks on U.S. ships drew the United States into the war. In April 1917 the United States declared war on Germany and joined the **Allies.**

In November 1917 there was a **revolution** in Russia. The old government was overthrown. The new government pulled Russia out of the war.

The United States declared war on Germany on April 6, 1917. Here soldiers say good-bye before leaving to go to war.

Word Bank   revolution   replacing a government with another one, usually by force

Germany's last chance

Germany had to win the war before the United States was ready to fight. With Russia gone, Germany could move more troops to the **Western Front**. On March 21, 1918, Germany attacked.

At first the Germans were successful. But in August 1918, the Allies drove the Germans back. U.S. fighting troops arrived at the front **line**. Germany's hope of victory began to fade.

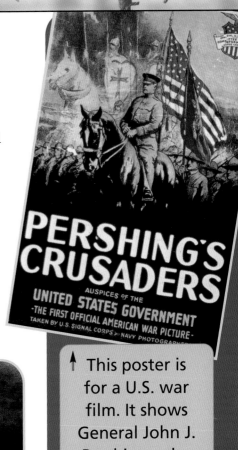

PERSHING'S CRUSADERS

AUSPICES OF THE

UNITED STATES GOVERNMENT

-THE FIRST OFFICIAL AMERICAN WAR PICTURE-

TAKEN BY U.S. SIGNAL CORPS AND NAVY PHOTOGRAPHERS

U.S. **artillery** fires at German **trenches** in September 1918.

↑ This poster is for a U.S. war film. It shows General John J. Pershing, who commanded the U.S. troops sent to Europe.

telegram   message transmitted by telegraph

Germany and Austria-Hungary collapse

Fresh U.S. troops had strengthened the **Allied** armies. Soon after August 1918, the German army began to collapse.

The Austro-Hungarian Empire also began to fall apart. Austria asked for peace on October 28, 1918.

Germany was in chaos. But German admirals in the navy did not want to give up. They tried to force the sailors to fight a last battle. The sailors refused.

Thousands of German prisoners were captured during the Second Battle of the Somme. This battle took place in August 1918.

German **prisoners of war (POWs)** march into captivity near Longpont in France. The year is 1918.

Word Bank   prisoner of war (POW)   soldier who is captured and put in prison by the enemy during a war

Rebellion

The German army also refused to continue fighting. Soldiers turned against their leaders. On November 7 these **rebel** soldiers took control of the German city of Munich. German leaders had to act fast to stop a **revolution**.

The German ruler, **Kaiser** Wilhelm II, **abdicated** on November 9. On November 11, 1918, the new German government agreed to peace. This agreement was called the **armistice**. The Great War was over.

Signing for peace

The armistice was signed in a railroad car parked near Paris, France. Marshal Ferdinand Foch (second from the right in the photograph below) represented the **Allies**. Matthias Erzberger and other politicians represented the Germans.

abdicate give up power or a position of power

A high cost

The war left Europe in a mess. More than eight million soldiers had died. Millions more were injured. The war had cost the **Allies** billions of dollars.

The Treaty of Versailles

In 1919 the Allies forced Germany to sign the **Treaty** of Versailles. The treaty was harsh. It took away lots of Germany's land. Germany was not allowed to have an air force. Its army was limited to 100,000 soldiers.

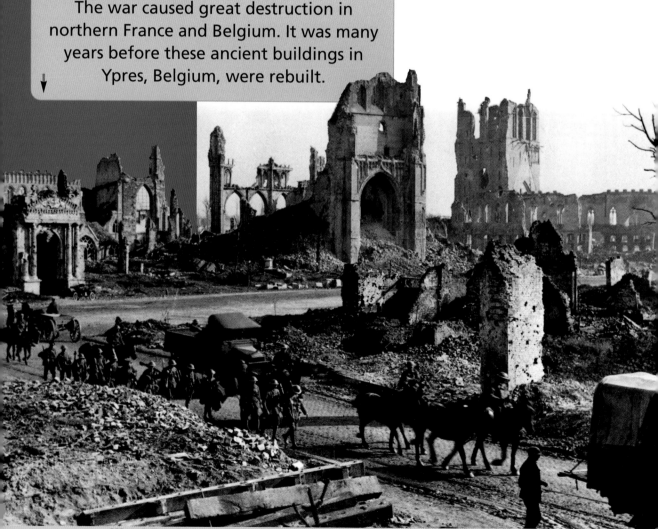

The war caused great destruction in northern France and Belgium. It was many years before these ancient buildings in Ypres, Belgium, were rebuilt.

Word Bank treaty agreement between two or more nations

The Allies also demanded huge amounts of money from Germany. This was to repay the costs of fighting the war.

Consequences

Many Germans were angry that their country had lost the war. Germany became very poor. This anger and poverty caused the Germans to elect Adolf Hitler to power in 1933.

Hitler promised to make Germany strong again. His attempt to do this started World War II in 1939.

This graveyard is for soldiers who died in World War I. There are many graveyards like this in northern France.

Adolf Hitler inspects German troops at Nuremberg in September 1935.

1914

June 28	Archduke Franz Ferdinand is killed by a Serb.
August 4	German troops **invade** Belgium.
August 7	British troops land in France.
August 31	Germany defeats Russia at the Battle of Tannenberg.
September 6	The **Allies** hit back at the Battle of the Marne.
October 15	A German attack is defeated at the First Battle of Ypres in Belgium.

1915

April 22	Germans use **chlorine** gas at the Second Battle of Ypres.
April 25	**Allied** soldiers land on beaches at Gallipoli in Turkey.

1916

January	Allies end the Gallipoli **campaign**.
February 21	The Battle of Verdun in France begins.
May 31	The Battle of Jutland keeps the German **fleet** trapped in the North Sea.
July 1	The Battle of the Somme in France starts. About 20,000 men are killed in one day.

1917

January 31	Germany announces its submarines will attack any ships helping the Allies.
March 17	**Czar** Nicholas, ruler of Russia, **abdicates**.
April 6	The United States declares war on Germany.
June 7	The Allies explode huge **mines** at Messines **Ridge** in France. They destroy the German defenses there.

November 6–7	**Revolution** breaks out in Russia.
November 20	British tanks are used in a surprise attack at Cambrai in France.
December 16	An **armistice** is signed between Russia and Germany, bringing peace between the two countries.

1918

March 3	Russia signs a peace agreement with Germany.
March 21	Germany launches a major attack on Allied forces along the **Western Front.** This attack was known as Operation Michael. The Second Battle of the Somme begins.
May 28	The U.S. army is victorious in its first major battle at Cantigny.
August 8	The Allies force Germany to **retreat** at the Battle of Amiens in France.
September 12	A second major victory for the U.S. army is won at the Battle of St. Mihiel in France.
September 27	The German **line** is broken by Allied attacks.
October 3	Germany approaches the United States to seek peace terms.
November 3	German sailors refuse to fight.
November 9	**Kaiser** Wilhelm II abdicates.
November 11	An armistice is signed between the Allies and Germany.

1919

June 28	The **Treaty** of Versailles is signed, officially ending the war.

FIND OUT MORE

Organizations

The Liberty Memorial Museum
This museum in Kansas City is the national World War I museum. It is the only museum in the United States dedicated to World War I, and it is also a memorial to those who served in the war. Exhibits include weapons, posters, uniforms, paintings, documents, and other historical objects. You can contact the museum at the following address:
100 West 26th Street
Kansas City, MO
64108

Books

Bosco, Peter and Antoinette. *World War I (America at War)*. New York: Facts on File, 2003.

Gilbert, Adrian. *Going to War in World War I (Armies of the Past)*. New York: Franklin Watts, 2001.

Saunders, Nicholas. *World War I: A Primary Source Material (In Their Own Words)*. Milwaukee: Gareth Stevens, 2005.

DVD/VHS

Films about World War I are often aimed at an adult audience. Ask a parent or teacher before watching these.

All Quiet on the Western Front (1930)
A German wants to fight for his country. But he learns that war is not glorious.

The First World War – The Complete Series (2005)
A ten-part documentary about the war that contains rare film.

World War I in Color (2003)
A six-part documentary with actual film of World War I and interviews with survivors.

World Wide Web

To find out more about World War I, you can search the Internet. Use keywords such as these:
- "Cambrai Offensive"
- World War I + trenches
- World War I + Eastern Front

You can find your own keywords by using words from this book. The search tips below will help you find useful Web sites.

Most sites are aimed at adults. They can contain upsetting information and pictures. Make sure that you use well-known sites with correct information.

Search tips

There are billions of pages on the Internet. It can be difficult to find exactly what you are looking for. These tips will help you find useful Web sites more quickly:
- Know what you want to find out about.
- Use simple keywords.
- Use two to six keywords in a search.
- Only use names of people, places, or things.
- Put double quotation marks around words that go together, for example, "Battle of the Marne."

Where to search

Search engine
A search engine looks through millions of Web site pages. It lists all the sites that match the words in the search box. You will find the best matches are at the top of the list on the first page.

Search directory
A person instead of a computer has sorted a search directory. You can search by keyword or subject and browse through the different sites. It is like looking through books on a library shelf.

GLOSSARY

abdicate give up power or a position of power

advance move forward

alliance two or more countries that have agreed to help each other in wartime

Allied belonging to the group of countries that fought together against Germany in World War I

Allies countries, such as Britain, France, the United States, and Russia, that fought together against Germany in World War I

ammunition bullets, shells, mines, and bombs

ANZACs Australian and New Zealand Army Corps

armistice ceasefire, or temporary halt to fighting

artillery large guns that fire shells or missiles

Austria-Hungary area in central Europe that consisted of Austria, Hungary, Bohemia, and parts of Poland, Romania, Slovenia, Croatia, and Italy

British Empire group of countries once controlled by Britain. In 1914, it included 25 percent of the world's land area.

campaign series of military operations during a war, all with the same purpose

Central Powers alliance of countries that included Germany, Austria-Hungary, Bulgaria, and the Ottoman Empire during World War I

chlorine greenish yellow gas that can kill people

clay smooth, almost waterproof mud

Czar name used for the rulers of Russia

dugout underground shelter dug by soldiers where they could rest in greater safety

Eastern Front battlefront between Germany and Russia

engineer person trained to build and repair things

fleet group of warships, or an entire navy

fortress specially strengthened building designed to defend an area in wartime

gas mask face mask with filters to remove poison gas

hard labor punishment that involves hard, physical work

invade enter a territory with armed forces, often to conquer that territory

Kaiser name used for the rulers of Austria-Hungary and Germany

line lines of trenches and other defenses

mine bomb left to explode later when something hits it or it is set off

no-man's-land unclaimed area of land separating enemies

Ottoman Empire large area of southwestern Asia, northeastern Africa, and southeastern Europe. Modern-day Turkey was at its center.

"over the top" phrase used to describe climbing out of a trench and moving into battle

peninsula piece of land with water on three sides

phosgene colorless poison gas that can kill people

prisoner of war (POW) soldier who is captured and put in prison by the enemy during a war

rebel person who fights against those who are in power

resource useful material, such as oil or metals

retreat move back

revolution replacing a government with another one, usually by force

ridge long, narrow hill

shell bullet-shaped bomb fired from a large gun

telegram message transmitted by telegraph

telegraph simple telephone that uses beeps for signals rather than voices

treaty agreement between two or more nations

trench long, narrow hole in the ground

trench foot breakdown of the skin inside wet boots, causing risk of infections

truce temporary agreement to stop fighting

Western Front battlefront between Germany and France